Walton We
the Ford, the Fc
the Foundry and the Prophet Elijah

Builders, architects and stone-carvers in an Oxford Victorian neighbourhood

John Sutton

Published by
Robert Boyd Publications
260 Colwell Drive
Witney, Oxon OX28 5LW

ISBN: 978 1 908738 32 5

First Published 2018

Printed and bound in the United Kingdom
by Henry Ling Limited
at the Dorset Press
Dorchester DT1 1HD

Contents

Walton Well drinking fountain.
(see opposite; also page 35 for original design of 1885)

Walton Manor: late Victorian development

The memory of Walton Well is preserved by the road of that name. But the well itself, together with the natural spring and ford right by it (at what became the junction with Southmoor Road), was effectively abolished in the early 1880s when it was drained and sealed below the improved cambered and metalled road leading to the canal, the railway crossings and Port Meadow beyond. This upgrading happened alongside the transformation of the surrounding area – all part of the extensive landholding of St John's College in north Oxford – from a patchwork of gardens, orchards, paddocks and scattered cottages into a residential suburb in response to increased housing demand in the City. Such an abrupt change of prospect from rural to urban, with streets lined by terraces of substantial brick houses, was only to be expected on this edge of the City's built zone which had already engulfed Walton Street and most of Jericho.

These developments had been foreshadowed in a way by the completion of the Oxford Canal as far back as 1790 along with the establishment of wharves for loading and unloading the narrowboats – carrying coal from the Midland mines in particular – and then, from the 1840s, parallel to the canal, the laying of railways (of two companies, in fact). This transport revolution not only expanded the reach of timber, quarried materials and other bulk industries supplying Oxford's busy building trade, but affected all sorts of ancillary services. Locally, such improvements included a swing-bridge over the canal at Walton Well Road to allow horse-drawn traffic access to the towpath as well as to Port Meadow and, by crossing the Thames at Medley weir and lock, to the farms on the Binsey side. Moreover, in 1886 the railway level-crossing, considered too dangerous with the sudden increase in people living and working so close, was replaced by a proper bridge. That, to this day, forms an extended hump to span the canal too. As a result, the run-off after occasional downpours, from the bridge itself combined with that from rooves and street gutters converging in the dip at a five-way junction, results in a drainage bottleneck. That is exactly where Walton Spring, Ford and Well had existed until 1880 – and where they are commemorated by a handsome and ornate drinking fountain, cut from blocks of Portland stone and capped by a dome.

This public installation of 1885 no longer functions to relieve the thirst of those who pass by (the Council having sealed the tap some years back). Yet, as a modest monument at this focal point, it is enough to catch the eye. Though standing only eight feet tall, being wedged between front-garden walls at the corner of Longworth Road, its neo-classical style adds a touch of variety to the dominant red-brick around it. And those who peer into the hollow structure may manage to read (if the angle of light is right), on an embossed copper plaque rivetted inside, the story of its erection and donation to the City.

That was an act of philanthropy by the ageing William Ward, a public-spirited former alderman who had twice fulfilled the role of City mayor some years before. Equally significant, he had done long service as chairman of the Corporation's Local Board, responsible for health regulations and all manner of public improvements. Ward had known this area from his boyhood, when it still had the feel of countryside. For his family had, over three generations since the opening of the Canal, accumulated its wealth as coal merchants with a wharf in Jericho and, by arranging for workers' housing to be built adjacent, as landlords too. It thus happened that when by the late 1860s bulk transport by canal was beginning to feel competition from the railways, the Ward family was able to excerpt a piece of their wharf area for the building of St Barnabas high-Anglican church whose conspicuous Italianate tower has ever since dominated Jericho and that stretch of the Canal.

Seen in this context, the provision of the fountain on the site of the former Walton Well might seem a minor gesture on William Ward's part. But it would have been an especially personal one for this City patrician, as he saw himself, and a way of ensuring – after having suffered some vindictive party-political bruising a few years earlier, resulting in his unceremonious ejection from the aldermen's bench – that he and his 'espousal of every good and useful work' in the City (as an obituarist put it in 1889) would be appropriately com-memorated.

The designing and unveiling of the Walton Well fountain in 1885 will be described in a later section of this booklet. Meanwhile, some background is offered on the streets of this neighbourhood, the area known as Walton Manor which was built up at the same time.

The Eagle Ironworks, 1820s to 2000

The Canal served perforce as the westerly limit of Walton Manor, just as it did already for Jericho, the suburb immediately to its south from which it was separated by the municipal cemetery (aptly named St Sepulchre) and the Eagle Ironworks. The latter consisted of the factory of William Lucy & Co which since earlier in the nineteenth century[1] (well before Lucy's own involvement) occupied the triangular space between its canal wharf, the cemetery and the track leading to the well and ford and beyond to Port Meadow. As a foundry in the first place, the Ironworks manufactured miscellaneous wares and fittings and, in particular, kept abreast of new municipal demands, in Oxford and elsewhere across the country, for such items as lamp-posts, railings and cast-iron drain covers for the streets (moulded with the Lucy name). In the twentieth century its specialisations shifted towards brass-smelting and -casting, especially for components of electrical switchgear for which demand was steadily growing both in Britain and for export overseas. (That change of emphasis was accelerated from 1960 after the firm's acquisition of Walton Meadow, between the canal and railway, which was developed into the factory's annexe, for assembling mains transformers among its finished products.)

But, eventually, as the twentieth century wore on, the firm recognised the unsuitability of persisting with busy manufacturing operations employing several hundred skilled staff in the midst of an urban residential area, and began a phased move from Oxford to new bases (some nearby in the county but others more distant, including scattered parts of Asia). Thus, in the 1990s the Walton Meadow annexe across the Canal was closed and sold for new housing (calling itself 'Waterside'), while in the following decade the whole factory complex lying behind Walton Well Road was demolished and replaced by blocks of modern flats and offices. A proportion of these flats, together with most of the original houses on Walton Well Road and others on adjacent streets, including Juxon Street on the Jericho side, remain the property of the Lucy firm and are administered by its property branch.

The spring, the well and the ford

Looking back beyond the 1880s, the Well of Walton – as far as one can tell from drawn sketches, passing allusions and a photograph by Henry Taunt – consisted of an open squarish trough, a few feet wide with stone-built sides and a neat flagstone border (and maybe a raised parapet on the upper side), designed to capture flow from a minor spring issuing from a patch of damp ground. It seems to have lacked any sort of cover or protective arrangement, while the excess from the spring was left to run unchannelled round the side and through the ford (or improvised stepping stones). This might have served as a useful wayside butt for carters' horses rather than a safe source of drinking water for people living nearby, let alone canal boatmen and foundry workers.

But more positively – before the installation of piped water hereabouts – this well was said to possess medicinal powers, for eye-sight especially, so that (as Ward himself recorded) 'children were brought before breakfast to have their eyes washed'. This salubrious reputation may, one suspects, have been borrowed in local lore from the more famous well and former shrine in Binsey churchyard associated with the legend of Oxford's patron saint, Frideswide, and the curing of blindness.[2]

St John's College, longtime landowner

At the time of the road improvements in preparation for house building early in the 1880s, with Walton Ford and Well both being drained and buried under the new street surface, the surrounding area was already regarded as beyond the bounds of Jericho itself. Calling it Walton Manor, or seeing it as just a part of that, was not exactly an invention, but neither was the neighbourhood precisely defined. Rather, it was generally understood (as it still is) as the space westward of Woodstock Road as far as the Canal which, with Kingston Road as its spine, was comprehensively developed for housing between the 1870s and 1890s. In fact, having been owned by St John's College for the previous three-hundred years – being part of the extensive St Giles fields, where ownership rights were regularised during the nineteenth century following parliamentary enclosure – it appears that the College itself (perhaps abetted by their architects publicising new house designs) revived the name 'Walton Manor' for this estate as lanes and boundary fences were being converted to metalled streets and formally named at the same time.[3]

This transformation by stages of North Oxford's fields to residential property was clearly in the College's long-term interest for ensuring a stable income for its statutory commitments and for playing its part in academic renewal at this time of modest rethinking of the University's role and appropriate reforms. That apart, there was broad public encouragement for property development, not least from the City's Corporation and the local weekly newspapers which provided regular reports on house building and improvements in this as in other parts of Oxford. The operation involved numerous small builders' firms and individual architects to whom leases were parcelled out by St John's bursar, but all subject to general planning conditions. Moreover the College as owner handled in advance the make-up of the streets with essential drains (and underground sewers too), and arranged with the City's water and gas companies to lay the mains to which the various builders could connect the new houses.

St John's architects, Wilkinson and Moore

The overall responsibility for the development of Walton Manor fell to St John's superintendent architect, William Wilkinson, who had earlier gained the trust of the College by surveying its property in Norham Manor (east of Banbury Road) and designing many of the elegant villas there. His reputation was established across the City too, not least for the fashionable Randolph Hotel built in the 1860s to face the Martyrs' Memorial and the breadth of St Giles Street. Being a bachelor, Wilkinson arranged, appropriately, to combine his architectural practice with his own residence next to the Randolph on Beaumont Street. Moreover, before planning the development of Walton Well Road and adjacent streets early in the 1880s, he brought his nephew, Harry Wilkinson Moore, into his team. This was more than a mere gesture of familial obligation on William Wilkinson's part, for Harry Moore was already demonstrating a flair for architectural draughtsmanship combined with an artist's eye for sketching and for thoughtful design of elevations with restrained decorative features. These talents were further encouraged as Moore took instruction at the new Ruskin School of Drawing – housed conveniently in the University Galleries (the Ashmolean Museum of Art and Archaeology, as it soon became) directly across the road from his uncle's practice. By 1881 Wilkinson, then in his sixties, was formally inscribing Moore, only half his age, as partner.

The whole Walton Manor operation was planned with thought for the needs of the different classes as recognised in the Victorian age – professional, moneyed, academic, trade, artisan, domestic service etc. In effect however, this did not amount to strict social zoning, since the terms of St John's building leases stipulated few specific controls. Nevertheless, it was obvious from the 1860s, as it still is, that the area between Kingston and Woodstock Roads was earmarked for the better-off and professional class who could afford the detached and the substantial semi-detached, four-storeyed houses erected there (the basements intended for servants) with spacious gardens in front as well as behind. By contrast, on the main part of Kingston Road itself where building was underway by 1870 – particularly the runs of 'model artisans' cottages' on the east side (designed by Clapton Crabb Rolfe, another nephew of Wilkinson) – the overall street scene looks denser and less leafy. And below Kingston Road the same applies to Southmoor and Walton Well Roads. Here all the plots were taken up quickly in the 1880s by a number of separate builders in what appears, nevertheless, to have been a coordinated exercise. Although these houses – in symmetrical pairs, foursomes or longer runs – do vary in size, few compare with the grander pairs and rambling 'villas' with their imposing doorways set in large gardens along the broad roads which run eastward of Kingston Road.

Such visible differences within Walton Manor notwithstanding, nowhere does one see 'two-up/two-down' houses so tightly packed as in the terraces of lower Jericho which had been built a few decades earlier, their front doors flush with the street. In fact, the development of the whole of Walton Manor – with the striking exception of the long plain terraces of Hayfield Road, a northward canal-side extension of Kingston Road designed by Harry Moore in the late 1880s to provide affordable accommodation for working-class tenants – ensured that each house, from the substantial semi-detached to the smaller terraced cottage with narrow back garden, was set back, if only a few feet, from the public way, while a low wall with railing helped ensure a sense of privacy. This insistence on a gated front yard, however narrow, for every artisan's family – together with bay windows (if only at ground level) and a porch covering the front door – reflects a mid-Victorian fashion change, in architectural tastes and concern for social standards alike. But, since so many of the houses, smaller as well as larger, or just floors or rooms within them, came to be rented out, with frequent change of occupants – and divided in ways that St John's and their architects could not have foreseen – this was hardly the dawn of the ideal of family home possession as came to be understood in the next century.

House interiors and later modifications

On glancing back to how these houses would have appeared when newly built in the late Victorian era, the differences would have been as much inside as outside, in particular the nature of essential domestic services. Although the laying of water and gas mains, and likewise of underground sewers, were by regulation included in urban street construction by that time, in the early phase of the development piped water would have reached only the ground floor or basement (or an annexe for a 'closet' at back), while coal for the fire-places had to be carried upstairs from a cellar or shed outside (either by servants occupying basements in the case of bigger houses, or by those who rented rooms). Only later as urban water pressure was increased, and gas became more adaptable for cooking and lighting or was later still replaced by electric power, was it feasible to install such amenities as toilets and kitchens upstairs as well as bathrooms fed by internal plumbing from roof tanks (with exterior down-pipes for the waste), let alone central heating (of even the crudest of sorts) and more efficient draught-proofing (of sash-window frames in particular).

Such improvements within the original Victorian brick structures have progressed decade by later decade, but mostly individually and haphazardly. (More coordinated improvements have occurred where blocks of houses were kept by St John's College for their own staff or, from the 1960s, by Lucy's – who bought whole blocks from the College as the original leases expired – in particular to accommodate their workers and families.) Brick chimney stacks, perched above the roofs and now redundant in so many houses, are a permanent reminder of previous living norms – as are the Victorian fireplaces in homes where successive owners have insisted on preserving them. And even where the fireplaces and grates have been ripped out or boarded up, and interior walls removed to increase living space (or the sense of it), the solid chimney breasts add some variation to the room shapes, and further provide useful alcoves – for fitting cupboards or bookshelves for academically inclined families. The fashion for such recent modifications, especially loft conversions and doubling of room sizes below by wall removal, would have been barely conceivable in the era before improved roof insulation and heating arrangements, let alone double glazing.

Changing streetscapes

Looking outside, the most conspicuous change around Walton Well since the Victorian era has been not to the built house fronts themselves but to the streetscapes nowadays accommodating motor traffic and parked cars. (Mercifully, however, almost all the gardens here are too small to be turned into gravelled forecourts for cars, as happens with more spacious properties of the north-easterly part of Walton Manor.) A particularly vulnerable feature, from a strict conservationist angle, has been the original sandstone kerb linings, many of which have splintered under the weight of commercial vans and lorries accessing these streets (for deliveries, removals and builders' materials, including regulation metal scaffolding each time a wall needs repointing or a roof repairing). Replacement of crumbling kerb steps now relies on concrete substitutes. Furthermore, and particularly striking when one glances at early photographs, is not only the empty appearance of the streets, save for the occasional horse-drawn cart or carriage, but equally the clear cambered road surfaces which were neatly separated by the kerb and gutter (with their cast-iron drain covers) from the pedestrian pavement. Another bane of parked cars in the modern age is, of course, their constant impediment to the Council's efforts to clear the gutters of mud, litter and autumn leaves!

One immediate and essential function of these roads when newly made-up in the 1880s was to ensure that the building operations proceeded smoothly, especially for the deliveries of bricks, timber and other materials by the wagon-load – indeed scores of them – during this very intense period of construction. Such heaps of materials deposited in the streets are shown on surviving prints from these early years of photography.

From the records kept by St John's College, the designs of many of the 1880s houses which were arranged in pairs or terraces on the streets towards the Canal radiating from Walton Well – namely Southmoor, Longworth and Walton Well Roads, together with filling the remaining gaps on Kingston and adjacent roads – are attributed to either Wilkinson or his nephew Moore, or simply to their joint practice. But it seems that Harry Moore's involvement was becoming dominant, as his distinctive style of gabled, red-brick, bay-windowed houses, with generous stone dressings and restrained decoration to the fronts and porches, developed with increasing confidence. That is evident on both sides of Southmoor Road where, once the street itself was laid out,[4] most of the basic structures (but not necessarily all interiors) of the hundred-plus houses were completed between 1882 and 1886. With various builders contracted, the work proceeded in patchwork fashion, while Moore, it seems, was keeping pace by developing his repertory of designs. These would have started at the north end with the terraces of identical and moderately sized three-storey houses on the east side, the style then being varied and enriched over the next couple or so years till the whole road was complete. Thus, the terraces became generally shorter towards the south end with the individual houses gaining in size (most having basements too, presumably intended for servants' accommodation, not to overlook the essential coal-shoots and, as noted, provision for washrooms and closets). Individual external details and stone-carved decorative devices (around doorways and their lintels and over sash windows) became more varied too. That trend was taken a step or two bolder as Moore then proceeded to design the more sumptuous houses at the northerly extension of Walton Manor (from St Margaret's as far as Frenchay Road).

The question of affordable accommodation

Although in later years Moore's relations with St John's soured somewhat, the Bursar berating him for indolence (or the inefficiency of the practice), his output in the 1880s, effectively creating this side of Walton Manor, had been energetic in the extreme. Even then, friction could arise between the College as patron and its area planner and chief architect. Notably, as work on Southmoor Road was starting in 1882, the Bursar expressed his concern on realising that Wilkinson and Moore were overstepping the College's intentions (if not specified instructions) by allocating plots for houses of more substantial size and higher lease values than working-class families could afford to rent. This complaint – regretting too the expense to the College of having laid out the public roads – sounds somewhat disingenuous, since the Bursar could not have been entirely blind to what was happening. Maybe his reprimanding letter was a way of deflecting blame after mutterings of dissent within the College – or a broader concern in the City – over a lax policy of property development which allowed commercial builders to exploit the opportunities for letting or onward sale of leases.

Following this bout of acrimony, the shortage of 'cottage' accommodation for the 'artisan' class was alleviated, if not perfectly satisfied, by Moore's designing the 'two-up/two-down' street-front terraces lining both sides of Hayfield Road, parallel to the canal and the coal wharves, which were still very active. That happened to be the nearest piece of St John's estate left available for the purpose by the mid-1880s. For that reason, the College varied its normal practice by leasing the land to a workers' building society but, at the same time, insisted on dictating its own architect's uniform design and appearance of both sides of the whole street.[5]

Harry Moore's redbrick signature

Hayfield Road was thus a special case. But overall, this Walton Manor enterprise of St John's College, as it developed from the 1870s, was much more than Wilkinson and Moore could handle alone, while the College was keen, for obvious financial reasons, to see the project moving forward and the leases sold. That meant that many plots or parcels were allotted to other architects, or to builders able to raise the capital or loans and competent enough to produce their own designs, some of them keeping the leases, usually for 66 or 99 years, on completion or selling on when convenient. But St John's retained the services of Wilkinson and Moore for approving the plans and elevations submitted (while everything had to pass through the City Engineer's department too). As a result the variety of styles and materials was controlled up to a point, and several of the independent builders apparently consulted Moore on plans and elevations or at least drew inspiration from his range – and his preference for red brick too. There is, thus, a measure of consistency of style, materials, spacing and overall appearance in these streets, but in a relaxed, not a strictly conformist, sense – or rather a 'character' as has been recognised more recently by their inclusion in the Victorian 'conservation area'. This principle of character is respected nowadays, more or less – if not to every purist's or objector's satisfaction – whenever applications for improvements, visible alterations or extensions at different levels are considered for planning permission.

Equally notable is that more than a century later when the Eagle Ironworks of W. Lucy & Co began moving its manufacturing operations away from Oxford so that the corridor between the canal and the railway could become available for house-building – beginning in the 1990s with the Waterside estate (after the demolition of Lucy's annexe),[6] that followed by William Lucy Way (on the 'island' dump site) – the dominant style was essentially a modified version of Moore's, albeit with fewer frills. Since access to this Waterside estate across the canal bridge (as also to William Lucy Way) requires passing through the streets which Moore himself had designed in the 1880s, it seems that this red-brick Victorian 'Gothic' style hung over the minds of the recent building firms – as well as those who were quick to buy these houses. At the same time, as Lucy's was transforming its main local business from manufacturing to property management (including long- and short-term letting), the firm undertook a purposeful improvement of its existing stock of Victorian-era houses on Walton Well Road and adjacent streets, by upgrading their general maintenance and internal amenities, with attention to outside appearances too. Altogether this reflected – and has doubtless helped propel further – the desirability of this post-industrial residential neighbourhood.[7]

Into the twenty-first century

It happens thus that Walton Well Road preserves most of its Victorian domestic architecture as well as vestiges of its industrial past, the former Eagle Ironworks. After the factory's demolition at the beginning of the present century and its replacement by modern blocks of flats as well as offices managed by Lucy's properties division, the firm, appropriately, reconstructed the gateway to the site and reinstated the stone-carved eagles perched as sentinels over it. Moreover, rather than erasing all memory of the location's industrial heritage, the names of the new apartment blocks facing the canal – Furnace, Fettler's and Foundry Houses – were chosen as a proud reminder of the company's manufacturing history encompassing almost two hundred years. On the question of maintaining the 'character' of the area and its residential component, the design and heights of these new buildings, as eventually approved after lengthy negotiations, seem to have fitted reasonably well, being largely hidden from view as one walks the old street.

The one building in the factory complex which survived the comprehensive demolition occupies the stretch of the south side of Walton Well Road next to the gate and eagles. This long plain construction of the 1950s – the least inspiring feature of the whole road – continues to serve as the Lucy firm's own offices together with the company boardroom. Ironically, the building of this administration block had involved destroying the oldest Victorian houses on the street, including the one where William Lucy installed himself with his family before his death from tuberculosis, aged only 35, in 1873. (While that ended the short Lucy connection with the firm, it's his name, fortuitously, that has stuck to this day.)

A residential suburb in an industrial environment

That house, built shortly before he died, would, together some shops on the opposite corner (of Kingston Road, as named later), have joined the few dwellings scattered about the area before both sides of Walton Well Road as far as the canal bridge were formally developed with substantial terraced housing in the 1880s, mostly to Harry Moore's designs. It is to that decade that the architectural heritage of this and adjoining roads belongs, with the houses on the south side of Walton Well Road serving as a partial curtain, shielding the factory's less elegant installations and activities from uninterrupted view from the street.

But the scene from the back windows of those houses – especially the terrace constructed of pale brick which was *not* designed by Moore – would have been every bit industrial. Moreover, those who chose to buy leaseholds or take lodgings here would have had to tolerate the noise of hammering and machinery, unloading of heavy materials from horse-drawn vehicles and likewise loading of products, let alone unhealthy coal-furnace smoke and soot. Such an intimate if tense social and environmental relationship between the factory and the surrounding community lasted for well over a century in which the foundry went through periodic innovations in its machinery and work practices in response to the changing markets for its products and a constant effort to maintain profitability (in times of war and peace alike).

Thus, in the 1960s, one way in which the management sought to boost efficiency and alleviate neighbourhood tension at the same time was by buying most of the houses on Walton Well Road, and also on Juxon Street (on the Jericho side), and several on Southmoor Road too – as the original leases from

St John's College were approaching their expiry – in order to accommodate a fair part of its workforce and their families. This was a rather unusual case of reversion, at a late stage in British manufacturing history, to a system more typical of the early Industrial Revolution whereby mill owners recruited manual workers by providing housing – whether out of enlightened benevolence or for sheer labour efficiency – 'at the factory gate'.[8]

The Elijah terrace, 1880s

The Elijah terrace on Walton Well Road (south side), designed by Joseph Curtis, 1882-85 (with Lucy & Co's 1950s office block adjoining at far end).

Two particular features of Walton Well Road, each bearing exquisite carved-stone relief decoration – and listed appropriately by Historic England (formerly English Heritage) – merit special attention here. One is the drinking fountain, already mentioned, which is perched on adjoining front-garden walls at the angle with Longworth Road. Though long decommissioned as a source of clear, clean water, it remains intact as a modest but handsome architectural monument, doubling as a memorial for the former well and ford.

The other special feature, virtually opposite on the south side of the road (now part of Lucy Properties' portfolio), is the compact terrace of eight identical slender houses distinguished by their prominent gables, slate roofs and bay fronts at ground level. These are built of pale yellowish brick, but with bands of bright, contrasting colours over the round-arched porches and sash windows with, for extra effect, dentilled bands under the eaves. Together with the diamond-patterned tiling of the front steps and porches, these touches relieve the terrace of what might otherwise seem a continuous monotone.

Moreover, each house displays in an arch over its first-floor window a rather

cramped *tympanum* (a lunette panel of carved stone) containing an un-mistakably biblical scene. That is for those curious enough to lift their eyes against the light to make out the intricate details of these reliefs (for which a pair of binoculars is recommended). The awkwardness of their position helps explain why this series has been known to some who regularly pass by without observing carefully (or even bothering to count) as the 'Twelve Apostles'. But anyone old enough to have been versed in the traditional rudiments of Bible knowledge at elementary or church school should quickly recognise these scenes (*nine* in all, the first house being double-fronted) – some featuring busy angels and each one the same venerable bearded old man – as illustrating the life of the Prophet Elijah, as told in the Old Testament *Books of the Kings* (the final chapters of *Book I* overrunning into *Book II*).

The exercise of identification has been eased in recent years since, after the closure of the ironworks and the brass foundry by stages, Lucy Properties as owner arranged for the whole terrace to be renovated, inside and out. As part of this face-lift the brick- and stonework were cleaned, and the accumulated factory grime which had obscured somewhat the life-story of the Prophet was carefully removed. Thus, with a bible at hand for chapter and verse, the tribulations and triumphs of Elijah's career have become manifest once more. (See the photographs and captions, p. 20-22.)

Since it is so individual architecturally, yet poorly recognised as such, we will look at this Elijah terrace first, and what can be gleaned about the careers of both the architect and the sculptor he engaged for illustrating these famous events in the Prophet's life. This assignment required a combination of artistic talent with technical skill for carving in relief. As for the reason for attaching such a bible story – a strip cartoon in effect – to a row of new houses in the 1880s not intended for any religious community or institutional use, but to be let to tenants at normal commercial rents, we can only speculate, and not very convincingly at that.

The architect, Joseph Curtis

The building lease for this terrace was negotiated with St John's College in 1882 by Joseph Codgbrook Curtis, an independent contractor with a flair for originality in his designs. Thus in press reports and on lithographic prints of his elevations he was routinely named as 'architect', although he consistently signed, listed and advertised himself simply as 'builder' (with his brother Charles as partner in the business and foreman at this point). While this may have been a case of modesty on Joseph Curtis' part – possibly he was self-taught and lacked a formal professional qualification – he seems, nevertheless, to have been a forthright personality with even a maverick streak. His previous commissions included runs of substantial houses elsewhere on St John's estate in North Oxford, and separately the Rewley House corner of Wellington Square when that site (previously occupied by the workhouse) was being redeveloped under the superintendence of the City's architect. His range extended further to city-centre department stores and Methodist chapels – the latter perhaps offering a clue to his religious inclination and the Elijah conundrum.[9]

With this reputation – some eccentricity in design notwithstanding – and useful operating connections in the local construction trade too, Curtis, one might suppose, would have proceeded with his concession on Walton Well Road without undue deference to St John's supervisor of the overall development of this part of Walton Manor. That was Harry Moore, whom Curtis may, very reasonably, have regarded his junior in the profession. In fact, Curtis' insistence on pale yellowish bricks and on slate for roofing – characteristics of all his work, apparently – appears almost as a deliberate trademark distinction from the typical redbrick and tiled designs of Moore and his contracted builders and less adventurous imitators, whose imprint was otherwise coming to dominate this and nearby streets. Moreover, Curtis had a personal interest in this terrace – particularly in the first house, the uniquely

Elijah in solitary exile – having fled from the wrath of King Ahab of Israel after prophesying the drought – being fed by the ravens (*I Kings 17*). One raven in flight above; the other, facing the Prophet and offering a loaf, has sadly lost its head.

Elijah and the widow who used her last handful of meal and drop of oil to bake a cake and relieve his hunger – and was miraculously rewarded thereafter as 'her barrel of meal and cruse of oil wasted not' (*I Kings 17*).

Elijah having fled for his life again – from the wrath of Jezebel, the queen, resentful of Elijah's victory over the 450 false prophets of Baal in the deadly sacrifice contest on Mount Carmel – sleeping under a juniper in the wilderness where he was eventually roused by an angel bringing sustenance (*I Kings 19*).

Elijah emerging from the cave where he had lodged forty days and nights, and the return of the angel bringing the word of the Lord – the 'still small voice' that followed the mighty wind, the earthquake and the fire – about his next assignment (*I Kings 19*).

Elijah casting his mantle upon Elisha whom he found 'plowing with his yoke of oxen' (*I Kings 19*).

King Ahab being confronted by Elijah in Naboth's ancestral vineyard – which the King had coveted and eventually seized, thanks to the stratagem of Jezebel to have Naboth falsely accused and stoned to death (*I Kings 21*).

King Ahaziah – successor to Ahab (killed in battle against the Syrians) – set on his bed after badly injuring himself in his palace (by falling 'through a lattice in his upper chamber'), and now being told by Elijah 'Thou shalt surely die' – due punishment for having sent first for help from Baalzebub, as if there were 'no true God in Israel' (*II Kings 1*).

River Jordan: Elijah, accompanied by Elisha, smiting the waters with his mantle so that 'they were divided hither and thither' (*II Kings 2*).

The other side: the chariot and horses of fire; Elijah already taken on board and ascending with two angels in attendance, and Elisha left standing and waving as the old Prophet's mantle drops to him (*II Kings 2*).

see note opposite →

double-fronted one, which he planned for his own use (maybe without revealing that intention beforehand). Thus, once that was ready in 1883/4, he moved in from his previous dwelling on Wellington Square.[10]

Work on the remaining seven houses on this Walton Well Road terrace then continued but with considerably less urgency, provoking St John's bursar to remind Curtis about honouring the agreed schedule and respecting the City's building regulations. This mild reprimand was followed by more pointed complaints about the unsightly appearance of the neglected construction site: it should 'look decent' and not be left unfenced as if 'anybody's rubbish dump'. There was a further reason for the Bursar's concern to present a respectable neighbourhood appearance, since at this point the facing plot was being prepared so that one of Moore's selected builders (Buckingham) could start work on the red-brick terrace of four (which bears the completion date '1885'), and prospective lessees would be coming to view. Despite Curtis' delays – whether because of illness or falling out with his brother who had been handling the labourers, or simply other priorities – the whole Elijah terrace was duly and neatly completed well within the decade.

Looking back at Joseph Curtis' career as builder-cum-architect in Oxford before this opportunity arose in Walton Well Road, his versatility and astuteness for architectural style and fashion, and equally for economy as dictated by clients, is nicely exhibited by the contrast between the two chapels which he designed. These were North Gate Hall (for the United Methodist Free Church) on St Michael's Street in 1870/71 (a building long closed as a place of worship with a schoolroom above, but surviving in, as Pevsner's guide puts it, a 'much mutilated' state, now housing a café); and secondly the (demolished) Primitive Methodist chapel in St Clement's parish (Rectory Road, formerly Pembroke Street), also of the 1870s. Thus North Gate Hall, just off Cornmarket, was built in stern nonconformist-classical style to fill a piece of street front which had fallen vacant, and was provided with a pediment on top and

---

What's not there.

Two of the most famous episodes in Elijah's life are, rather surprisingly, not illustrated among these nine scenes (although both are on Benson's wish-list for SS Mary & John: see p. 26). These are the reviving of the widow's son (*I Kings 17*), and Elijah's resounding defeat of the prophets of Baal on Mount Carmel (*I Kings 18*), that event being followed by the cloud no bigger than a man's hand rising from the sea and thickening to a black sky heavy with rain to relieve the drought. (Both episodes are treated dramatically in Mendelsson's oratorio *Elijah*, popular with choirs and their audiences.)

Rewley House, corner with Wellington cartouche

prominent stone facings cleverly diverting attention from the structure's cheaper pale brick; whereas the design for the Primitive Methodists of East Oxford was Victorian Gothic *à la mode*.

Moreover, wherever it seemed appropriate, Curtis delighted in artistic touches with increasing boldness. At Wellington Square he took up the incoming fashion for decoration in stone-carved reliefs by having them run in raised bands, together with spandrels, over the lintels and porches of the six substantial houses designed as a continuous block around the (everted) corner which forms Rewley House.[11] The subjects of these reliefs – more easily appreciated after their recent cleaning – range from humorous and grotesque to profane and pagan, including griffons, male and female heads capped, hooded and crowned, as well as Green Men and Bacchi with vines, trees and flowers in abundance.

More serious on this square – named to commemorate the Duke of Wellington, not so much for his military victories and occasional role as prime minister, as for a lengthy stint of elder statesmanship as Chancellor of the University – Curtis (presumably with the City architect's approval) inserted high on the corner house (where it is easily overlooked) a cartouche of the Iron Duke himself.

The sculptor, Samuel Grafton

For undertaking these embellishments, including the Wellington cartouche, Curtis engaged a stone sculptor, Samuel Grafton, who operated from the Cowley Road area, then a suburb of rapid development for light industries and working-class accommodation. In time he settled at the corner of Union Street, and may have had his workshop there, while he upgraded his listing from 'wood and stone carver' to 'architectural and monumental sculptor'. For satisfying Curtis' requirements and mildly eccentric tendencies, Grafton was clearly a competent craftsman who could combine technical expertise with artistic sensibility, enough to distinguish himself from any run-of-the-mill mason or tombstone engraver. Elsewhere around the City, Grafton's work can be seen above the shop fronts on the corners of King Edward Street and the High – another example of bands of humorous figures (modified somewhat in recent restoration) – and the larger heads and other features derived from riverine lore which cap the arches on both faces of Magdalen Bridge (after its widening in 1883).

A few years earlier Grafton had been contracted for sculptural details of the new church of St Mary and St John on Cowley Road, notably on the east front (Christ on high), and undertook detailed work in the chancel too, especially the canopies over the sedilia, for which he was duly commended in the press. That ecclesiastical experience might have been a consideration when Curtis turned again to Grafton, ten years after their collaboration at Wellington Square, for executing the Elijah scenes on Walton Well Road.

An aborted scheme on Cowley Road: SS Mary and John church

This merits a digression – albeit with the risk of stretching speculation. The construction of this High Anglican church, which was intended to serve the new but poorly endowed parish of Cowley St John, advanced necessarily by stages under the determined leadership of the vicar, Fr Richard Meux Benson (the founder of the Cowley Fathers' seminary close by). The chancel, with Grafton's work inside and out, was given priority (late 1870s). But the Gothic nave had to wait a few years for adequate funds; and the prominent tower was added later still, while several details on Benson's ambitious plan, both within and out, were abandoned permanently. Nevertheless, in time for the consecration in 1883 – and the first baptism, for which the water was specially drawn and carried from the River Jordan no less! – a programme of stone-carved biblical scenes was set in motion at the west end of the nave, along the walls and on the pillar capitals and the corbels supporting the arches. While no confirmation seems to have survived that any of these carvings, like the chancel work, were by Grafton's hand, it might be guessed from the style.[12]

It is worth lingering awhile in the nave of SS Mary and John (the Evangelist) to take stock of what was – and what was not – completed of Benson's grand design. His vision (as described in the parish magazine for November 1883) was that the whole interior should 'speak of God's work in nature and in grace'. For this purpose he selected over sixty stories from the Old Testament for the pillars, with as many more to follow from the New Testament, while the Nine Orders of the Heavenly Host were to oversee it all from on high – at an estimated cost of £20 for the four sides of each capital. Thus, the carvings began, appropriately, with instalments from the Book of *Genesis* (the Creation to Noah), as well as a few random scenes from *Prophets* and *Kings*. But then, as happens, the money ran out and the initial fund-raising enthusiasm with it, so that the larger part of the scheme was never executed. The Prophet Elijah, naturally, was on Benson's wish-list, meriting four scenes (meant, doubtless, to be carved around a single square capital). These absent scenes were to include the ravens and the Prophet's 'translation' to heaven – both of which turn up on the Walton Well Road terrace.

So – to conclude the digression – Grafton may well have been suffering disappointment at the loss of a lucrative commission on Cowley Road at the very time that he answered Curtis' invitation to bring the Bible to Walton Manor. Further, so one might suggest, he would have come with images in his head of scenes from the life of Elijah, which of course needed adapting from church pillars and corbels, as intended by Benson, to *tympana* on otherwise normal house fronts. But the idea behind the scheme was certainly Curtis' own in the first place. That is evident on the architectural elevations which he had already submitted to the City Engineer's office for approval, clearly marking these half-moon panels to be filled in some artistic way.

Bible consciousness and business opportunities

For Curtis, perhaps more than Grafton, was definitely Bible-conscious. This might be inferred from his readiness to design nonconformist chapels (as noted above); but it is revealed in a more definite but odd manner in a long-winded letter for the *Oxford Chronicle* (14 October 1865), contributing to a tedious running debate over the Local Board's bye-law proposals on privies, water-closets, drains, sewers, cesspools and ash-pits. The subject was one on which Curtis, as a builder acquainted with the practicalities of providing essential sanitary amenities for town houses (and the costs of complying with newfangled regulations), felt himself qualified to offer advice. Yet curiously, to introduce his intervention, he thought it appropriate to admonish readers of 'an old book', somewhat neglected though it may have become in many a home, but still containing an abundance of 'good and great maxims' supposedly relevant to the issue at hand!

The collaboration of Grafton with Curtis on Walton Well Road continued after completing the Elijah terrace. For at the top end, towards the junction with Walton Street, a few houses in yellow brick on either side bear all the marks of Curtis' design and Grafton's stone-relief carving. These attributions are definitely documented for the largest, most prominent and flamboyantly decorated house hereabouts – 'extravagant', as the architectural historian, Andrew Saint, described it – with the name 'Holyfield' engraved over its grand front door. That merits a short study of its own (in the section below).

At the same time one wonders who was the sculptor of the pair of stone-cut eagles perched above the Ironworks' gates as if to vet everyone passing through.[13] (Following the recent transformation of the site, with the factory giving way to flats and offices, these eagles have been thoughtfully reinstated over the main entrance.) Samuel Grafton's work again? Having professionally handled both wood and stone in his career, he would have been conversant with eagles as required for church lecterns.

His name and fame as a stone-sculptor have not, in studies of Oxford Victorian architecture, endured like that of the O'Shea brothers who worked on the face of the University Museum in the late 1850s (with the encouragement of John Ruskin advocating the revival of Gothic architectural forms together with appropriate decoration). But Grafton would doubtless have seen the work of these pioneers and been inspired by it. Indeed, if one were searching for a model for the gifted stonemason Jude ('the Obscure') of Thomas Hardy's novel written only a few years later, Grafton might well fit the type – except that he worked from Cowley Road, not lodging in Jericho within sight of St Barnabas' tower as the fictional Jude Fawley did on arriving in Oxford with an unrealistic career ambition. Like Jude, Grafton suffered marital difficulties – going through divorce and remarriage, an experience not so usual for his class and time. On the other hand, he does not seem to have shared Jude's recurrent neuroses or chronic unreliability about work commitments![14]

Why Elijah?

The question of why Joseph Curtis, the architect, chose to adorn the Walton Well Road terrace with the frieze of scenes from the life of Elijah was left unanswered above. There have, of course, been rumours or ingenious guesses over the years. These are recorded here but with the caution that, unless more explicit evidence from the 1880s comes to light, they can carry little conviction.

Since this terrace was not intended for a religious community or an educational benefaction in the 1880s – in fact it seems that Curtis, as already noted, was planning from the start to reserve for himself the first house, while retaining the lease of the rest for letting to tenants as a personal investment – one naturally wonders what motivated him to embellish the whole front with an extended bible story. And why Elijah? One rumoured explanation (if not mere invention) is that this was Curtis' way of giving thanks to the Lord after one of his family fell seriously ill, only to recover in answer to prayer when virtually at death's door. The account of how Elijah, 'the man of God', miraculously revived the poor widow's son whom she had given up for dead (*I Kings* 17) might have encouraged this theory – except that this famous episode in the Prophet's life is one, rather surprisingly, not illustrated in this series. (Might raising from the dead have seemed too contentious an issue at that time?)

Another and more far-fetched speculation would relate these carved reliefs to the building lease which Curtis obtained from St John (*Baptist*)'s College, seeing that the various anecdotes about John the Baptist told in the Gospels – his abode in the wilderness and frugal, foraging diet, his reverence for Jordan's water and call for repentance while prophesying Christ – portray him as if Elijah reincarnate. (There are reasons for treating this theory sceptically. The letters from St John's bursar at the time of building, periodically berating Curtis – as already noted – for sloth and a casual attitude towards the lease agreement and Council regulations, let alone allowing rubbish to accumulate on the unfinished site, suggest that business relations were not of the friendliest.)

Speculate as one may, Joseph Curtis' motive for fitting this moral, biblical cartoon-strip onto a new residential terrace will probably remain unknown – other than his respect for the word of the Bible, as already recorded, and his willingness to design Methodist chapels. But what is certain about his planning of the Walton Well Road terrace is that he had decided before laying the foundations to insert something decorative if not actually artistic in the nine *tympana* (lunette panels) on the house fronts. That intention was very clearly marked on the elevations which he submitted for the City Engineer's approval beforehand. He had a personal interest in mind too, since he kept the lease of the whole terrace of eight houses once they were ready for occupation, letting seven of them to tenants while, as seen, reserving the larger double-fronted one for himself. It remained his home (and the address of his business) for 17 years – till he died there, aged 81, in 1902.

Wear and tear

Like all artistic commissions of this sort, the basic intention and the positioning of the work would have been dictated by the architect beforehand. But it's likely, of course, that the designs were sketched in outline and discussed between Curtis and Grafton before the latter began carving the scenes in stone. (That was doubtless done in the workshop, after which the panels would have been carted across Oxford, ready for lifting by ladder and cementing into the nine *tympana*.) Looking at the panels now, more than 130 years after, one may discern gaps or imperfections. But, on closer examination, these result from weathering and unfortunate breakage of delicate detail, as happens over time wherever intricate carvings are exposed to the elements. Notably, there is an embarrassing void in the middle of the first of the nine scenes, where the ravens are feeding Elijah in the wilderness. But, after focussing the binoculars, it transpires that the head of the bird delivering a loaf to the Prophet's hand has simply fallen off. Similarly in no.6, where Elijah the trouble-maker confronts the wicked King Ahab in Naboth's vineyard (which the latter had coveted and eventually seized, thanks to the treacherous machinations of Queen Jezebel), the drama of righteous accusation and indignant denial is lost since one raised arm of the prophet, and likewise of the king, has broken away. On other panels the damage – lost fingers and whole hands, of both the Prophet and attendant angels – may escape the notice of most who pass by.

Such inevitable wear apart, the question of the artistic merit of this series of panels must be left to those who stop to admire (or evaluate critically) this example of Victorian heritage. Whatever the verdicts, these Elijah scenes were patently the product of a pair of hands skilled in working stone in relief and conversant with the broad conventions of biblical imagery followed in that era. The assignment demanded an eye for balancing detail in each confined semi-circular panel, with flowers, palms and other vegetation filling the corners or branching overhead. But Grafton as sculptor was no slave to bland fashion. Each panel needed original thought (rather than being copied from a standard trade manual or template). There is a sense of purpose and activity, especially in the expressions on the angels' faces as they rouse the famished, exhausted

Elijah (crying 'It is enough') from his refuges in the wilderness; or again, where Elisha, while busy ploughing his furrow with yoked oxen, is summoned by the senior prophet to a swift change of career. (That it's the wrong model of plough for that part of the world at that time doesn't matter!)

Holyfield House, 1891

This imposing double-fronted residence, which surpasses any other on Walton Well Road in both size and decoration, was built by Curtis in 1891 for a Thomas Johnson[15] with whom the architect appears to have been well acquainted in business. For Johnson, who listed himself in the directory as wheelwright, was employed at Lucy's as 'iron-master', meaning, apparently, the foreman of the workforce if not effective manager of the factory's day-to-day operations. For this reason, so it seems, he felt the need for a house which would make a statement at the front of the Eagle Ironworks, dominating the junction of Walton Street with Kingston and Walton Well Roads at the same time.

The one difficulty, however, must have been in arranging the space for anything so ostentatious, especially since Johnson was including in his lease

Holyfield House (corner Walton Street and Walton Well Road)

Walton Well Road, view from Walton Street end, c 1900, showing Holyfield House
(left) with iron balcony bedecked with plants. (Taunt Collection 11455,
copyright Oxon. History Centre)

two more houses on the downhill side (filling the space to the factory gate and
the eagles) as part of the same construction job. Thus Holyfield House, instead
of standing proud and free, is actually attached on that side to these two
relatively modest houses of Curtis' inimitable style (including his trademark
yellowish brick and Grafton's carving of the stone dressings). More than that,
the attachment is not at a rightangle.[16] Equally oddly, if one glances round the
unattached corner of the big house, the angle measures less than a right-angle,
so that the shape of the whole structure is essentially rhomboid; that required
some clever internal adjustments (a skewed plan, which is so obvious on
walking through the wide front door). One might imagine Johnson having sat
down beforehand with Curtis, as an architect settled next to the works and
capable of solving awkward problems of this sort. In the event, a separate,
private, access (with, originally, its own iron gate at the street) was arranged
on the free side with a very respectable second 'front' door under a deep arched
porch, indicating that Johnson commissioned this house to combine under one
roof the works' offices at front with his family residence above.[17]

Characterising Holyfield House as 'extravagant' (as Andrew Saint did in
passing) is justified not just by its size (four floors including basement) but
also by its classical pediment with pineapple finials and profuse rosette
decoration, its twin bays and wide sash windows for spacious rooms inside,

and a studded front door approached up steps and flanked (rather in-congruously) by polished porphyry columns; and above those, with, over the threshold, a *tympanum* of garishly coloured glass between Grafton's stone-carved spandrels.[18] And, though the basic structure of the house consists of Curtis' standard pale brick, it's the matching stone facings, together with Grafton's various touches at different levels upwards, that exude an impression of something grander.

Walton Well drinking fountain, 1885

Although it is no longer connected to the mains water supply, this elegant feature, designed in 1885 by St John's architect, Harry Moore, remains as a protected monument at the site of the former ford and well. It was constructed from blocks of Portland stone, with a miniature dome over the basin and a striking finial – in the form of a votive vase or funerary urn – on top.[19] The body of the fountain was neatly positioned (by the mason, James Clifford of St Aldates) between the front walls of the pair of substantial houses being built at the same time, while the sculptor (McCulloch from London) completed the details and profuse decoration exactly to Moore's plan.[20] Thus, despite its modest size, being barely eight feet tall, and its 'Grecian renaissance' style (as the press described it) contrasting with the new environment of predominantly red-brick housing which Moore and his builders were creating all around, the fountain fitted into the overall neighbourhood prospect. It remains (as Andrew Saint commented) the 'focal point' of the three streets converging here (or *four* if one includes the gap left between the houses opposite the fountain for secondary access to the Eagle Ironworks). Its formal presentation to the City would have doubled in a way as an inauguration for this latest area of development on St John's College estate.[21]

The donor and city patrician, William Ward

The fountain was intended to be more than a work of art, of course, but to fulfil a useful, charitable purpose for all who passed by either for work or for leisure on the way to Port Meadow. It was commissioned as an act of philanthropy – or, rather, a combination of munificence and personal pride – by William Ward (1807-1889) who had served the City of Oxford for many years as alderman and twice as mayor (1851 and 1861). Being both a leading businessman and a prominent High Churchman with a big family house on St Giles, he cultivated in his advancing years the air of a senior City father and the consummate patrician. As already noted, the family had been established in Oxford since 1790 when his grandfather set up in Jericho as a wholesale coal merchant, taking advantage of the completion of the Canal which assured faster and cheaper transport from the Midland mines. For improved efficiency, as their business prospered, the Wards saw the advantage of building labourers' accommodation on land they had acquired adjoining the Jericho wharves. And when, in 1869, a new church was needed for the increased population of that suburb (more than St Paul's on Walton Street could accommodate), William

Walton Well drinking fountain, designed by Harry Moore and presented to the City in 1885: Moore's lithograph (from *Building News*, 16 Dec. 1887: *copyright* British Library)

Ward and his brother Henry were able to spare a plot by the canal for the building of St Barnabas.

That charitable act was, doubtless, broached by Thomas Combe – the superintendent of the nearby University Press, the foremost employer in Jericho – who shared Ward's high Anglican leaning and was wealthy enough to underwrite the building of the new church. There was probably little need to prompt, since the Ward family tradition of paternalist promotion of healthy religious instruction for the working class stretched back at least thirty years; for it was Ward's father, Henry, who had provided the boatmen's floating chapel and school on Castle Mill Stream, right by Hythe Bridge and the canal-end basin.[22]

William Ward's continuation of his family's commitment to good works, sound learning and godliness included benefactions to local schools as well as founding a Sunday school at St Giles (the original parish church for the whole of north Oxford, fields and all, where he served as churchwarden). More influentially, he had chaired for several years the Corporation's Local Board, the body responsible for health, streets, improvements, building regulations and public services (everything down to the sewers) across the City. He also sat – as if by right, or so it looks in retrospect – on numerous governing boards, benches and commissions: Canal Company, City magistrates and tax commission, the Radcliffe Infirmary on Woodstock Road and the Warneford Hospital in Headington, as well as the Diocesan Church Building Society.

The St Barnabas project thus arose at the right time to engage Ward's energies and public standing, for it coincided with his falling foul of the dominant Liberal faction in the Corporation. Apparently, his manoeuvres to promote a suitable Conservative candidate to stand to represent the City at the next parliamentary election proved just too clumsy, so that his opponents responded in equal measure by voting him off the aldermen's bench.[23] After this wounding experience he forswore further holding of office, preferring instead to be respected as a grand old City Father (one punctilious in attendance at the annual Corporation service in the City Church, St Martin's at Carfax).

The dedication and inscription

Returning to the fountain itself, the text of the inscription – embossed on the copper plate fixed above the spout inside the fountain's hollow stone structure – was approved, or more probably dictated, by Ward himself and then passed to Moore who, as a formality, cleared it together with the architectural details at the City Engineer's office before work commenced:

Walton Well drinking fountain: the inscription bolted inside, below the dome.

With the consent of the Lords of the Manor [i.e. St John's College] *this drinking fountain is erected by Mr. William Ward to mark the site of a celebrated spring known as Walton Well adjacent to the ancient fordway into Port Meadow called Walton Ford*

with the year *1885* included above and, around the margins, a biblical invocation:

Drink and think of him who is the fountain of life (a twist of a famous verse in the *Book of Revelation:* 21.6).

If this wording has a rather pompous ring for modern tastes, it is in keeping with inscriptions in general of the Victorian age recording charitable works.

The presentation of the fountain to the City by Ward in person – in a ceremony on site on 3rd September 1885 – was reported in the Oxford weekly newspapers, with speeches printed at tedious lengths, as was typical of the time.[24] Despite the chosen day turning horribly wet, so that everyone attending

Walton Well drinking fountain: photo early 20th century, showing 'Grecian' finial (removed mid-late 20th century) (Taunt Collection, Oxon.CC 56_734, *copyright* English Heritage).

the event, whether out of duty or mere curiosity, was anxiously glancing around for shelter, protocol had to be respected. Thus the donation[25] was graciously accepted by the chairman of the Local Board who offered suitably complimentary comments, so that the donor himself, almost eighty years old and virtually blind, could be assured that everyone looking on appreciated the fountain's 'chaste', 'tasteful design and elegant workmanship'. It merely awaited connection to the City's 'good and wholesome' piped water – as promised by the Waterworks. (Ward would have been heartened to know that it is now protected as a listed monument, even if no longer active as a fountain.)

In response Ward took the opportunity to share his still vivid reminiscences of Walton Manor as it had been during his boyhood – a rural outskirt of the City with a few spaced cottages attached to orchards, paddocks and small-holdings. That was before the railway age and the need for the extended humped bridge, over both the canal and the rail tracks, on the way to Port Meadow. He recalled in particular the former well and ford just where he was standing, as well as the parish pound (for errant livestock) which had, until

Walton Well drinking fountain now, less the finial.

only a couple of years before the transformation of the area, continued to function within a small fenced enclosure immediately behind where his new fountain was now emplaced.

The survival of a local monument

From its erection in 1885 till the present day, this fountain turned monument has endured remarkably well, despite its exposure to an industrial environment for most of that time, and nowadays to a moderately busy suburban road junction. On at least two occasions it has received attention from the works department of the Corporation or Council. First, in 1906/7, there is a record of the structure being 'rebuilt' for some reason; if one takes that literally, its restoration to Moore's original design was remarkably meticulous on every detail. Perhaps that report was alluding to some minor necessary adjustments – a repair or improvement of the piped water supply, say? Secondly, some unspecified modifications were undertaken in 1975,[26] which may have involved cleaning the stonework and (perhaps not entirely judicious) the application of yellow paint or preservative to the stonework which, despite some fading, remains visible in patches. This may have been the occasion when the fountain was decommisssioned as such and the tap sealed, with the water pipe at the back being cut away. However, the photographic record shows that the removal of Moore's Grecian finial from the dome had occurred before that date.

Now, almost half a century since that latest attention, for good or otherwise, the fountain could benefit from careful cleaning and filling of cracks (including the finial's amputation scar on the dome). Moreover, the projecting rim of the basin needs some infilling after having suffered, late in the last century, a couple of hits by lorries reversing from the factory gate opposite. (There is better protection now, since the erection of traffic bollards at this junction and the Council's planting of a pair of maples at the millennium. The latter, however, need regular trimming, since they arch over the monument, while their leaf stains require periodic cleaning.) More particularly, the copper inscription plate has long needed secure rebolting – it appears there was a botched attempt to heave it off some years ago. One other detail sadly missing – a successful case of metal theft – is the original brass or copper lionhead cover over the tap and spout, as devised by Harry Moore in 1885.

Notes

1   The earliest evidence for what was at first called the Jericho Iron and Brass Foundry on this site is about 1825. The date '1760', as claimed on the former back gate to the works on Juxon Street, seems spurious – as the company itself admits: see *The Lucy Story*, ch.2.

2   That historic well, named in versions of the same legend for St Margaret of Antioch, was recalled to public notice by its restoration and stone inscription in 1874 (preceded by a Burne-Jones pre-Raphaelite window in Christ Church Cathedral), that is a few years before the erection of the fountain at Walton Well. By then Binsey's 'treacle well' figured in Charles Dodgson (*aka* Lewis Carroll)'s popular *Alice in Wonderland*.

3   St John's left its imprint in this exercise, with many of the new streets being named after rural manors and parish advowsons held by the College. While some of these are quite distant from Oxford, others are much closer, notably a cluster of villages on the old Berkshire side of the Thames – Longworth, Fyfield, Southmoor and Kingston Bagpuize/(St John) Baptist.

4   The line of Southmoor Road followed an older track with rails laid for horse-drawn carts carrying sand and gravel, quarried in particular from the area of Chalfont Road and required for stable underlay of the railways. This railed track – as shown on photographs – turned by Walton Well to cross the muddy ford and the canal draw-bridge.

5   See Hinchcliffe, p.81-4.

6   This is the former Walton Meadow which Lucy's acquired in 1956; the firm then expanded an existing 1930s-style storage building to house the assembly plant. A few years later a works bridge over the canal was added, connecting with a tunnel under Walton Well Road, to ease transport of metal scrap, foundry products and assembled equipment by forklift trucks between the two sites of its operations. These complicated arrangements, which still required use of the public road for its noisy lorries and the taller, heavier, rattling forklifts, became a running cause of strained relations with residents of the immediate neighbourhood.

These relations had already been soured by the 'sea of concrete' which was deposited over 'many acres' of this former meadow in 1957/58 to enable open storage of materials and works vehicles (and, subsequently, a lorry park). As a fait accompli, this action was highlighted among residents' complaints. At the subsequent public enquiry some minor details of mitigation were won (in particular concerning the height of the proposed

canal-side boundary wall and protection of the towpath willows). But the
'sea of concrete' remained until the 1990s when Lucy's sold Walton Meadow,
with a permit for change of use, to Berkeley Homes for building the
Waterside estate.

7   The air-quality has improved too – at least its visible signs, with less soot
settling on windows, their frames and sills.

8   The Eagle Ironworks, from the early nineteenth century till the end of the
twentieth, might offer itself as an ideal objective case-study for a keen
student of labour and social history – to complement the company's own
business history, *The Lucy Story* (see Bibliography).

9   However, Curtis' name does not figure on surviving registers of local
Methodist congregations (kindly checked by Rev. Dr Wellings), so it could
be that these building contracts were simply offered to him as the best the
chapel elders could afford. He may, perhaps, have belonged to some other
nonconformist congregation, as one might imagine from his Bible-
consciousness, noted below.

10 It was at Wellington Square, a decade before this move, that Curtis set a
precedent for himself. Having been allocated in the early 1870s the building
lease for six contiguous houses to fill the corner now comprising Rewley
House (the University's Centre for Continuing Education), he started with
the most southerly one (which adjoins, without any gap, the straight line of
St John Street) since he was reserving it for himself. More than that, he
prepared his plan and front elevation to include two front doors, but at
separate levels, so that his highly productive colleague in the building trade
– John Dover who had handled the basic construction of North Gate Hall
for Curtis and was now working separately on another side of Wellington
Square – could share this large house.

Before construction had reached the top storey, the *Oxford Chronicle* (12
October 1872) reported its 'prepossessing appearance', with the further
comment that 'Mr. Curtis has not been careful to adhere to any strict style
of architecture, but only to avoid, so far as possible, a violation of the laws
of construction.' Reading between the lines of this tortuous sentence, one
senses that Curtis was playing a game with a callow reporter who, anxious
for a correct statement with the necessary jargon straight from the horse's
mouth, had his question thrown back as he was shown the drawn elevation
of the whole house. That would have illustrated the upper half awaiting
completion, with a tower above the main porch, to be 'finished with a spire
roof and ornamental finial.' The contrast with the long, plain-fronted

terraces of St John Street, built in a late Regency style a generation before, to which Curtis was physically attaching his avant-garde house (at the line of the demolished workhouse wall), would have struck anyone passing by.

[11] Though thoroughly altered inside, the original exterior remains largely unaltered, except for the modern face of no.2 which serves as the entrance to the Continuing Education complex.

[12] It is recorded, however, that a London mason, McCulloch, was also involved. As noted below, the same McCulloch was two years later engaged by Harry Moore for the detailed relief carving on the Walton Well fountain (just when Grafton would have been completing the reliefs for the nine Elijah *tympana* directly across the road).

[13] There is a rumour that these are not the original eagles but replacements for an earlier pair in terracotta which were stolen. If so, the theft (or just breakage?) of the terracotta must have occurred long ago, since the existing stone eagles look to have weathered a good century of outdoor exposure.

[14] Samuel Grafton appears not to have been related to the two Charles Graftons (father and son) who managed and owned (in whole or part) the Eagle Ironworks in the middle part of the nineteenth century when the firm called itself successively 'Grafton & Hood', 'Grafton & Company' and 'Grafton & Lucy' till, some years after Grafton junior's death (and Lucy's also), it became simply 'William Lucy & Co'.

[15] This Thomas *Edwin* Johnson should not be confused with another Thomas Johnson who was locally well-known in the late nineteenth century as a coal merchant and beer retailer, for whom the equally substantial (but now demolished) Navigation House was built by Aristotle Bridge and the canal wharves at the south end of Hayfield Road: see Davies and Robinson, p.14.

[16] The front doors of these two attached houses are visibly offset to correct the angles inside.

[17] The side/back wing has been extended secondarily, both outwards and upwards.

A stone fixed to this side of the house bears the date *1891* and the name of *Alan J.H. Johnson*. Presumably this was a son, who in time became an estate agent and was sometimes listed with his names spelt out in full, *H* being for 'Holyfield' – a family or maternal name? – the same as that engraved over the front door. He continued living in Holyfield House till 1920, but then moved to the far end of Walton Well Road when the family residence was taken over by the Catholic Workers' (Plater) College.

Later, after mid-century, Lucy's acquired this house for its social club, a gesture appreciated by many of its staff who were accommodated by the company in the nearby streets. Later again, in the 1990s, as the Lucy firm was running down its industrial activity in Oxford and turning over most of its site for housing, Holyfield House was appropriately occupied by an estate agency which took advantage of the marketing of new properties being built by Berkeley Homes on the former Walton Meadow, which had till then served as the factory's annexe just across the Canal.

[18] These spandrels have suffered weathering of the relief details over time, but have also been obscured by an equally ornate wrought-iron balcony (very likely made to order in the Eagle works) which was fitted immediately above them. At first sight this balcony might be mistaken as a verandah for sitting out. But on second look, it would be ridiculously narrow and unsafe – doubly unsuitable in fact, since the only access would have been by climbing through the central first-floor window! The real purpose of this balcony and its railing was – as a photograph in Taunt's postcard series reveals – to support extra adornment in the form of sprawling and climbing plants and for hanging other floral arrangements over the front steps too. It was clearly an afterthought to Curtis' design, yet a feature added quite early in the house's history. One unfortunate result of securing this iron structure over the porch was that the ends of Grafton's bands of stone relief had to be rudely sacrificed.

Even now, long since the display of *live* vegetation on the front of Holyfield House, the tastefully designed ironwork seems to fit rather well into the overall 'extravagance'. But that was achieved at a further expense to Grafton's delicate production of *stone-relief* vegetation on the spandrels above the door, simply because the iron frame cuts out the light. While the matching cornucopias and massed floral designs may, despite their weathering, be fairly easily made out, the pair of youthful musicians happily fiddling and piping away on either side are virtually lost amongst this profusion of vines, acanthus leaves, marigolds etc. They are best revealed by taking close-up flash-photos.

[19] This finial was removed within living memory, presumably for safety concern, leaving a cement-filled scar. If it is still locatable, it might be safely restored to its rightful place alongside other minor repairs and due conservation work. For proof of the finial's existence, see Taunt's photograph (early twentieth century), showing precise agreement with Moore's lithograph of 1885 (next note).

20 This survives as a lithograph illustrated in the trade magazine, *Building News*, as a special encomium for Moore two years later (though unfortunately the editor misread Moore's handwriting and, doubly confused, attributed the work to 'H. Wilkinson, Dover'!).

Moore's training at the Ruskin School, and experience in Oxford as an apprentice in his uncle (William Wilkinson)'s practice, would have acquainted him with neo-classical designs, including domes and cupolas, albeit of grander scales (e.g. The Queen's College).

A quip overheard from one of the mason's team – that their job was to cover the old well 'with a fireplace to keep it warm' – would have suggested by the form of the half-dome wrought-iron canopies being installed over fireplaces in the main rooms of neighbouring houses then under construction.

21 As Ward acknowledged in his speech, 'St John's gave the ground' – a space measuring barely three feet by four at the street corner!

22 That beneficence was directed at the navigation community of itinerant narrowboat hands and wharfside families who felt shy of joining the congregations of the City's established parish churches and chapels. It may well be that the eventual decay and sinking of the boatmen's chapel in 1868 helped spur the planning of St Barnabas' church. See Davies and Robinson, p.44-6.

23 These events were reported at length in the Oxford weekly newspapers and were recalled in detail on Ward's death twenty years after, in particular by the *Oxford Times* which at that period maintained a noticeably Conservative sympathy.

24 At that date newsprint technology had not developed sufficiently to regularly include photographs of events, and reporters relied on copying verbatim and straight dictation.

25 No mention was made of the expense covered by Ward; but the professional fees as well as labour and material costs must have been substantial. Blocks of Portland limestone would, doubtless, have been available locally in builders' yards, as surplus from more substantial projects in the City and University.

26 This date coincides closely with the designation of the conservation area. Since the monument was formally listed as 'historic' in 1972, there should be an official record of these 'modifications' or conservation measures – and, with luck, of where the missing finial was stored.

Bibliography

This booklet makes no claim to being a fully definitive study of Walton Well itself, together with the neighbouring streets and their architectural history. While efforts have been made to check details and background, certain points of accuracy, omission or alternative interpretation will doubtless be identified. Readers so interested might be encouraged to correct or offer deeper insights.

Detailed (academic-style) referencing is deemed unnecessary for an account of this sort. The following works are listed for sources and background:

Tanis Hinchcliffe, *North Oxford* (Yale U.P. for St John's College, Oxford) 1992, with numerous photographs – covers the College's estates and their 'development' in late nineteenth century

Andrew Saint, 'Three Oxford architects' in *Oxoniensia* (journal of the Oxford Architectural and Historical Society) vol. 35, 1970, p.53-102 – the careers of William Wilkinson and his nephews, Clapton Crabb Rolfe and Harry Moore

Tony Winckworth with Mike Hobbs, *The Lucy Story: portrait of a family company* 2009 – produced by Lucy&Co (and incorporating materials from an earlier company history: P.W.S. Andrews and Elizabeth Brunner, *Eagle Ironworks,* 1965, and M.G. Thatcher's updating of 1994, *A most interesting company*)

Ann Spokes Symonds, *The changing faces of North Oxford* (*Book Two*) [Walton Manor] 1998 – useful for photographs, old and recent, and various characters and anecdotes

Mark Davies and Catherine Robinson, *Our Canal in Oxford, from Wolvercote to Jericho and the City* (Towpath Press) 1999 – well researched with valuable details and illustrations

Peter Howell and Andrew Saint, *Notes on Victorian architecture in Oxford* (collected typescripts 1970-73, related *inter alia* to the conservation area and its extension: Oxfordshire History Centre)

Geoffrey Tyack, *Oxford, an architectural guide* (OUP) 1998 – handy for reference

Acknowledgements

The author thanks the following for assistance: Thomas Alexandridis, all photographs (except those in Henry Taunt collection); Gordon Geddie, genealogy searches; Mark Hilton and Linda Wastie, Lucy Group; the archivist, St John's College; Martin Wellings, Methodist records; Rosy Hancock, SS Mary&John church; Lambeth Palace archives (Bermondsey), records of Society of St John Evangelist (Cowley Fathers); British Library, newspaper depository (Colindale); Oxford City Council offices and Oxfordshire History Centre for assistance with various records, photographs, microfilms/fiches etc.

Parts of this account incorporate materials already used in short articles published in the *Oxford Times* monthly magazine for June 2013, and in *Jericho Matters* issue 35, December 2017.

The author is indebted to the Greening Lamborn Trust for a generous grant towards the cost of printing and publication of this book.